THANKS
FOR BEING A
Friend

Thanks for Being a Friend

©2004 ELM HILL BOOKS
ISBN: 1-40418-5321

Manuscript written and compiled by Rebecca Currington in association with Snapdragon Editorial Group, Inc.

Cover and Interior design by JacksonDesignCo, llc

Introduction

Thanks for Being a Friend has been created in celebration of the role our friends play in our lives. It is intended to serve as a simple and earnest word of thanks for all the love, loyalty, and laughter they continue to provide for us through the years.

As you read, we hope you will be moved to outwardly express your love and respect for the special friends who have graced your life. Honor them for sticking with you through good times and bad. Assure them that they can depend on you to do the same. And thank God for the gift that keeps on giving—the love of a true friend.

The Publishers

Friendship *n.*: a state of mutual affection and regard between two people.

Table of Contents

A friend is one who knows you as you are

Understands where you've been

Accepts who you've become

And still, gently invites you to grow.

The Nature of a Friend

Put your life on the line for your friends.

——— ✳ ———

JOHN 5:13 THE MESSAGE

*L*ife without a friend

is like life without the sun.

———✳———

GERMAN PROVERB

Friends are the sunshine of life.

JOHN GAY

From acquaintances,
we conceal our real selves.
To our friends we reveal
our weaknesses.

———※———

BASIL HUME

There's a special kind of freedom
friends enjoy—freedom to share
innermost thoughts, to ask a favor,
to show their true feelings,
freedom to simply be themselves.

I always felt that the great high privilege,

relief and comfort of friendship

was that one had to explain nothing.

——— ✳ ———

KATHERINE MANSFIELD

To know someone here and there
who thinks and feels with us
and who, though distant, is close to us
in spirit, makes the earth a garden.

———— ✳ ————

JOHANN WOLFGANG VON GOETHE

A real friend warms you by his presence,

trusts you with his secrets,

and remembers you in his prayers.

Many might have failed
beneath the bitterness of their trial
had they not found a friend.

CHARLES SPURGEON

It is one mark of a friend

that he makes you wish

to be at your best

while you are with him.

———✳———

HENRY VAN DYKE

I love you not only for what
you have made of yourself,
but for what you are making of me.

ROY CROFT

*F*riendship is a plant

that must often be watered.

——— ✳ ———

GERMAN PROVERBS

Friendship without self-interest

is rare and beautiful.

JAMES BYRNES

If you have one true friend,

you have more than your share.

———✳———

THOMAS FULLER

*Being with you is like walking
on a very clear morning—
definitely the sensation
of belonging there.*

———✳———

E. B. WHITE

When a friend asks,

there is no tomorrow.

A true friend thinks of you
when others are thinking of themselves.

A friend is someone
you can do nothing with
and enjoy it.

———*———

THE OPTIMIST

One is taught by experience
to put a premium on those few people
who can appreciate you for what you are.

——— ✳ ———

GAIL GODWIN

I will gladly share with you your pain,

If it turns out I can no comfort bring;

For 'tis a friends right,

Please let me explain,

To share in woeful as in joyful things.

———✳———

GEOFFREY CHAUCER

The Comfort of a Friend

*God comforts us every time we have trouble, so that
we can comfort others when they have trouble.*

——— ✳ ———

2 CORINTHIANS 1:4 NCV

*Y*ou talk about your pleasures

to your acquaintances;

you talk about your troubles

to your friends.

———※———

FATHER ANDREW

No problem is ever as dark
when you have a friend
to face it with you.

 riends add a brighter radiance

to prosperity and lighten the burden

of adversity by dividing and sharing it.

——— ✳ ———

CARDINAL RICHELIEU

Friendship doubles our joy
and divides our grief.

———— ✳ ————

FRANCIS BACON

A real friend is one who walks in

when the rest of the world walks out.

———✳———

WALTER WINCHELL

A friend will joyfully sing with you
when you are on the mountain top,
and silently walk beside you
through the valley.

———— ✳ ————

ARISTOTLE

We do not so much need

the help of our friends as

the confidence of their help in need.

———*———

EPICURUS

A friend in need is a friend indeed.

—✳—

ENGLISH PROVERB

When true friends meet

in adverse hour,

'Tis like a sunbeam

through a shower.

——✳——

SIR WALTER SCOTT

When a friend is in trouble,
don't annoy him by asking
if there is anything you can do.
Think up something appropriate
and do it.

———— ✳ ————

EDGAR WATSON HOWE

*T*here are moments in life

when all that we can bear is the sense

that our friend is near us.

——— ✳ ———

HONORE DE BALZAC

In times of great anxiety
we can draw power
from our friends.

D. LUPTON

There are friends who sail together,

Through quiet waters and stormy weather,

Helping each other through joy and strife.

They are the kind who give meaning to life.

The Loyalty of a Friend

A real friend will be more loyal than a brother.

✳

PROVERBS 18:24 NCV

*F*ew delights can equal

the mere presence of one

whom we trust utterly.

———— * ————

GEORGE MACDONALD

A loyal friend laughs at your jokes
when they're not so good,
and sympathizes with your problems
when they're not so bad.

———※———

ARNOLD H. GLASOW

*F*riendship implies loyalty,

esteem, cordiality, sympathy,

affection, readiness to aid, to help,

to stick, to fight for, if need be.

———✳———

B. C. FORBES

We have been friends together

in sunshine and in shade.

——— ✳ ———

CAROLINE NORTON

We can never replace a friend.

No one has a double in friendship.

——✳——

JOHANN SCHILLER

This one for Linda

I have friends in overalls
whose friendship I would not swap
for the favor of the kings of the world.

THOMAS A. EDISON

*L*ove is swift, sincere, pious, joyful,

Generous, strong, patient, faithful,

Prudent, long-suffering, courageous,

And never seeks its own;

———✳———

THOMAS À KEMPIS

The Love of a Friend

Friends love through all kinds of weather.

❋

PROVERBS 17:17 THE MESSAGE

I have learned that

to have a good friend

is the purest of all God's gifts,

for it is a love that has

no exchange of payment.

———✳———

FRANCES FARMER

If we would build on a sure foundation
in friendship, we must love friends
for their sake rather than for our own.

———— ✳ ————

CHARLOTTE BRONTË

The impulse of love that leads us

to the doorway of a friend

is the voice of God within.

———✳———

AGNES SANFORD

So long as we are loved
by others, I would almost say
that we are indispensable;
and no man is useless
while he has a friend.

ROBERT LOUIS STEVENSON

*F*riendship is in loving
rather than in being loved.

———✳———

ROBERT BRIDGES

Friendship's a noble name,
'tis love refined.

——— ✳ ———

SUSANNAH CENTLIVRE

I breathed a song into the air,

It fell to earth, I knew not where;

For who has sight so keen and strong,

That it can follow the flight of song—

The song from beginning to end,

I found again in the heart of a friend.

HENRY WADSWORTH LONGFELLOW

The Heart of a Friend

Jesus says, "I have called you friends."

❋

JOHN 15:15 NKJV

We cannot tell the precise moment

when friendship is formed.

As in filling a vessel drop by drop,

there is at last a drop which makes it run over.

So in a series of kindnesses there is,

at last, one which makes the heart run over.

———✳———

JAMES BOSWELL

In friendship we find
nothing false or insincere;
everything is straightforward
and springs from the heart.

CICERO

*F*riendship that flows from the heart

cannot be frozen by adversity,

as the water that flows from the spring

cannot congeal in winter.

———*———

JAMES FENIMORE COOPER

After the friendship of God,

a friend's affection

is the greatest treasure here below.